The Littl
of Sand and

Ideas for activities for the Foundation Stage

by Sally Featherstone
Illustrations by Michael Evans

LITTLE BOOKS WITH **BIG** IDEAS

Featherstone Education
An imprint of Bloomsbury Publishing Plc

50 Bedford Square
London
WC1B 3DP
UK

1385 Broadway
New York
NY 10018
USA

www.bloomsbury.com

Bloomsbury is a registered trade mark of Bloomsbury Publishing Plc

Text © Sally Featherstone, 2002
Series Editor, Sally Featherstone
Illustrations © Michael Evans, 2014
Cover photographs © Shutterstock

British Library Cataloguing-in-Publication Data

A catalogue record for this book is available from the British Library.

ISBN: 978-1-4729-1284-8

Library of Congress Cataloging-in-Publication Data
A catalog record for this book is available from the Library of Congress.

1 3 5 7 9 10 8 6 4 2

Printed and bound in India by Replika Pvt Ltd

This book is produced using paper that is made from wood grown in managed, sustainable forests. It is natural, renewable and recyclable. The logging and manufacturing processes conform to the environmental regulations of the country of origin.

**To view more of our titles please visit
www.bloomsbury.com**

Contents

Introduction

This book is one of the titles in a series of Little Books, which explore aspects of practice within the Early Years Foundation Stage in England. The books are also suitable for practitioners working with the early years curriculum in Wales, Northern Ireland and Scotland, and in any early years setting catering for young children.

Across the series you will find titles appropriate to each aspect of the curriculum for children from two to five years, giving practitioners a wealth of ideas for engaging activities, interesting resources and stimulating environments to enrich their work across the early years curriculum.

Each title also has information linking the activity pages to the statutory early years curriculum for England. This title has been updated to include the revised Early Learning Goals published by the Department for Education in March 2012. The full set of 19 goals is included in the introduction to each book, and the activity pages will refer you to the relevant statements to which each activity contributes.

For the purposes of observation and assessment of the children's work in each activity, we recommend that practitioners should use each of the 'revised statements' as a whole, resisting any impulse to separate the elements of each one into short phrases.

The key goals for this title are highlighted in blue, although other goals may be included on some pages.

PRIME AREAS

Communication and language

(1) Listening and attention: children listen attentively in a range of situations. They listen to stories, accurately anticipating key events and respond to what they hear with relevant comments, questions or actions. They give their attention to what others say and respond appropriately, while engaged in another activity.

(2) Understanding: children follow instructions involving several ideas or actions. They answer 'how' and 'why' questions about their experiences and in response to stories or events.

(3) Speaking: children express themselves effectively, showing awareness of listeners' needs. They use past, present and future forms accurately when talking about events that have happened or are to happen in the future. They develop their own narratives and explanations by connecting ideas or events.

Physical development

(1) Moving and handling: children show good control and co-ordination in large and small movements. They move confidently in a range of ways, safely negotiating space. They handle equipment and tools effectively, including pencils for writing.

(2) Health and self-care: children know the importance for good health of physical exercise, and a healthy diet, and talk about ways to keep healthy and safe. They manage their own basic hygiene and personal needs successfully, including dressing and going to the toilet independently.

Personal, social and emotional development

(1) Self-confidence and self-awareness: children are confident to try new activities, and say why they like some activities more than others. They are confident to speak in a familiar group, will talk about their ideas, and will choose the resources they need for their chosen activities. They say when they do or don't need help.

(2) Managing feelings and behaviour: children talk about how they and others show feelings, talk about their own and others' behaviour, and its consequences, and know that some behaviour is unacceptable. They work as part of a group or class, and understand and follow the rules. They adjust their behaviour to different situations, and take changes of routine in their stride.

(3) Making relationships: children play co-operatively, taking turns with others. They take account of one another's ideas about how to organise their activity. They show sensitivity to others' needs and feelings, and form positive relationships with adults and other children.

SPECIFIC AREAS

Literacy

(1) Reading: children read and understand simple sentences. They use phonic knowledge to decode regular words and read them aloud accurately. They also read some common irregular words. They demonstrate understanding when talking with others about what they have read.

(2) Writing: children use their phonic knowledge to write words in ways which match their spoken sounds. They also write some irregular common words. They write simple sentences which can be read by themselves and others. Some words are spelt correctly and others are phonetically plausible.

Mathematics

(1) Numbers: children count reliably with numbers from 1 to 20, place them in order and say which number is one more or one less than a given number. Using quantities and objects, they add and subtract two single-digit numbers and count on or back to find the answer. They solve problems, including doubling, halving and sharing.

(2) Shape, space and measures: children use everyday language to talk about size, weight, capacity, position, distance, time and money to compare quantities and objects and to solve problems. They recognise, create and describe patterns. They explore characteristics of everyday objects and shapes and use mathematical language to describe them.

Understanding the world

(1) People and communities: children talk about past and present events in their own lives and in the lives of family members. They know that other children don't always enjoy the same things, and are sensitive to this. They know about similarities and differences between themselves and others, and among families, communities and traditions.

(2) The world: children know about similarities and differences in relation to places, objects, materials and living things. They talk about the features of their own immediate environment and how environments might vary from one another. They make observations of animals and plants and explain why some things occur, and talk about changes.

(3) Technology: children recognise that a range of technology is used in places such as homes and schools. They select and use technology for particular purposes.

Expressive arts and design

(1) Exploring and using media and materials: children sing songs, make music and dance, and experiment with ways of changing them. They safely use and explore a variety of materials, tools and techniques, experimenting with colour, design, texture, form and function.

(2) Being imaginative: children use what they have learnt about media and materials in original ways, thinking about uses and purposes. They represent their own ideas, thoughts and feelings through design and technology, art, music, dance, role-play and stories.

Sand and water are frequently found in early years settings, but often are neglected as areas of the foundation curriculum. They are thought of as background activities, often taken for granted and missed when practitioners are evaluating the quality of their setting and planning for the day or the week.

Sand and water play has associations with holidays, seaside fun, parks, countryside, streams and rivers. It offers children endless opportunities to recreate and imagine, and to explore and begin to understand the texture, movement, properties and features of two of the most common natural substances in the world. Well-managed sand and water areas encourage children to develop fine motor control, sociability, co-operation and imagination.

Children will frequently choose sand and water over other activities in free choice sessions, and their play in these areas is often unaccompanied and unobserved by adults – except, of course, when the water gets on the floor, or the sand gets in someone's hair!

However, if the selection of tools and toys children find when they embark on the activity is limited and the organisation of the activity confused and difficult to manage, the inspiration for constructive play will be missing. The result can be aimless activity where children are 'coasting' without learning, or frustration with limited resources resulting in inappropriate or anti-social activities.

Management and organisation

Well-managed and well-organised sand and water areas offer children significant opportunities for learning using familiar materials and tools. They can also be the starting point for exploring themes, small world play and investigating a variety of scientific concepts.

Whatever the size or type of your setting, sand and water should be consistently offered to the children. In settings where space is limited, water play can be provided in a washing up bowl or the sink, and sand play in a cement mixing tray or a large plant tray, plastic box or bowl. Wherever possible, both activities should also be available outside, using trolleys, tables or simply positioned on the grass or play area.

It will be helpful if the toys and equipment are stored on shelves or in baskets near the activities, with simple labelling or matching shapes on the shelves to enable children to get things out and put them away independently. The water and sand trays should usually be empty of toys and equipment at the start of each session, allowing children to select the equipment they wish to work with. When working on a thematic session, a table or basket next to the tray or bowl can contain the objects offered for the current focus.

A simple plank across a sand or water tray is helpful during play for resting containers while they are filled, and for providing temporary storage for toys and equipment during a session.

Some questions for practitioners

It might be useful to ask yourselves the following questions when considering sand and water play in your setting:

▶ Is the area attractively laid out, with signs, notices and suggestions?

▶ Are there sufficient resources – enough water or sand, enough toys, different sizes of containers etc?

▶ Are the toys and equipment attractively arranged and stored so children can get them out and put them away easily?

▶ Are the toys and equipment of good quality and in good condition – would you want to play with them?

▶ Are the sand and water areas changed frequently by adding new things, making suggestions, changing the location or the appearance of the sand/water – changing the colour, moving objects in or around the area, or adding things that make children think?

▶ Is the sand and water play offered both indoors and out?

▶ Are aprons and other protective clothing available and easy to put on, take off and hang up?

▶ Do adults spend time with these activities, valuing them and observing what happens, making suggestions and playing alongside the children? If this never happens, the children will get a strong message that sand and water play are just 'keep busy' activities with no value to adults.

All at sea

Turn your water tray into a sailing experience by creating boats of all sizes and types. Go on holiday, carry cargo or visit other lands and islands across the sea!

Contribution to Early Learning Goals

PRIME

Communication and language
① Listening and attention
② Understanding

Physical development
① Moving and handling

Personal, social and emotional development
① Self-confidence and self-awareness
② Managing feelings and behaviour
③ Making relationships

SPECIFIC

Mathematics
① Numbers
② Shape, space and measures

Understanding of the world
② The world

Expressive arts and design
① Exploring and using media and materials

What you need:

- water tray, bath tub or other receptacle
- assorted small toy boats
- toy bricks or lego to make into islands or harbours
- plastic sheeting to cover islands or make beaches
- string to join boats
- paper and sticks to make sails
- materials to make your own boats
- play people or other miniatures for sailors
- fish and other sea creatures

Vocabulary

- sea
- land
- dock
- harbour
- sail
- fishing
- cargo
- ropes
- journey
- captain
- crew
- anchor
- country
- abroad
- different
- weather
- travel
- luggage
- ticket
- cabin
- holiday
- map
- telescope
- island

Other ideas

- Add some blue or green food colouring to the water.
- Using a selection of materials, encourage the children to create their own boats and blow them across the water. Have a race!
- Load the boats up with any cargo you can find. Make cranes for the docks.

Songs and stories

- A Sailor went to Sea, Sea, Sea
- The Big Ship Sails
- Row, Row, Row your Boat
- The Lighthouse Keeper's Lunch
- The Little Boat
- Mater Salt the Sailor
- Sailor Bear

Pond life

Explore a pond. Create a toy pond in a water tray, tub or paddling pool, or make a real pond using a sheet of black pond liner.

Contribution to Early Learning Goals

PRIME

Communication and language
① Listening and attention
② Understanding
③ Speaking

Physical development
① Moving and handling

Personal, social and emotional development
① Self-confidence and self-awareness
② Managing feelings and behaviour
③ Making relationships

SPECIFIC

Mathematics
② Shape, space and measures

Understanding of the world
② The world

Expressive arts and design
① Exploring and using media and materials

What you need:

For a toy pond:

▶ a water tray or paddling pool

▶ plastic bugs, beetles, frogs, butterflies, dragonflies etc.

▶ plastic ducks and fish

▶ stones, gravel and pebbles

▶ plastic pond weed and lily leaves

▶ logs, twigs and sticks

▶ green or blue food colouring

For a more realistic pond:

▶ pond liner

▶ bricks or bags of sand to prop up the edges

▶ real pond plants (or plastic ones from an aquarium shop)

▶ nets and magnifying glasses

▶ a water lily

▶ real pond water

> I will need

Vocabulary

▶ water	▶ hover	▶ smaller
▶ under	▶ wings	▶ grow
▶ on top	▶ legs	▶ leaves
▶ surface	▶ eggs	▶ roots
▶ swim	▶ tadpoles	▶ catch
▶ hop	▶ hatch	▶ feet
▶ fly	▶ magnify	▶ fins
▶ jump	▶ bigger	▶ breathe

Other ideas

▶ Hatch frog spawn.

▶ Go pond dipping.

▶ Freeze small plastic bugs in ice cubes and float them in the pond.

▶ Cut floating lily leaves from thin green plastic.

▶ Create your own flying creatures to hang on strings above the pond.

Songs and stories

▶ 5 Little Speckled Frogs

▶ 5 Little Ducks Went Swimming One Day

▶ Nine Ducks, Nine

▶ The Hungry Caterpillar

▶ Tiddalik

▶ Non-fiction pond life books

▶ Life cycle books such as: From Tadpole to Frog

Go fish!

Get up to all sorts of fishy business with this fun game. Add to the challenge by keeping scores!

Contribution to Early Learning Goals

PRIME

Communication and language
(1) Listening and attention
(2) Understanding
(3) Speaking

Physical development
(1) Moving and handling

Personal, social and emotional development
(1) Self-confidence and self-awareness
(2) Managing feelings and behaviour
(3) Making relationships

SPECIFIC

Mathematics
(1) Numbers
(2) Shape, space and measures

Understanding of the world
(2) The world

Expressive arts and design
(1) Exploring and using media and materials

What you need:

- a paddling pool, bowl or water tray
- plastic fish of all shapes and sizes
- other plastic water creatures such as crabs, lobsters, octopuses and ducks
- bamboo poles and string
- permanent markers
- clipboards or whiteboards for scoring
- bowls to collect your 'catch'
- food colouring
- a small magnet or magnet strip

Vocabulary

catch	net	shell
count	team	line
score	different	magnet
how many	size	string
water	colour	winner
hook	scales	more
turn	skin	less

Other ideas

- Create some aquariums from shoe boxes with cellophane fronts. Make fish and plants from card, then colour and hang them inside.
- If possible, have some real fish in your setting! Goldfish are good value, but make sure they have enough room in their bowl or tank.

Songs and stories

- 1, 2, 3, 4, 5, Once I caught a fish alive
- One Fish, Two Fish, Red Fish, Blue Fish
- The Rainbow Fish
- Commotion in the Ocean
- Over in the Meadow

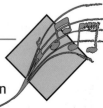

Freezing cold

Experience life in arctic lands by transforming your water tray into a polar bear environment. Make `icebergs' in the freezer, or use crumpled paper or card.

Welcome to the Antartic

Contribution to Early Learning Goals

PRIME

Communication and language
1. Listening and attention
2. Understanding
3. Speaking

Physical development
1. Moving and handling

Personal, social and emotional development
1. Self-confidence and self-awareness
2. Managing feelings and behaviour

SPECIFIC

Mathematics
2. Shape, space and measures

Understanding of the world
1. People and communities
2. The world

Expressive arts and design
1. Exploring and using media and materials
2. Being imaginative

What you need:

- ▶ a water tray, bath or other receptacle
- ▶ Arctic and Antartic animals – e.g. polar bears, penguins, seals
- ▶ small world people
- ▶ card, small boxes etc to make sledges and boats
- ▶ white painted wood and polystyrene to make icebergs
- ▶ ice cubes or small slabs of ice
- ▶ blue or green food colouring

If you want to be strictly accurate, remember: penguins and polar bears live at opposite ends of the Earth!

Vocabulary

- ▶ sea
- ▶ land
- ▶ ice
- ▶ iceberg
- ▶ fish
- ▶ catch
- ▶ float
- ▶ sink
- ▶ freeze
- ▶ underwater
- ▶ swim
- ▶ growl
- ▶ flipper
- ▶ egg
- ▶ feathers
- ▶ fur
- ▶ skin
- ▶ boat
- ▶ sledge
- ▶ igloo
- ▶ house
- ▶ snow
- ▶ husky dog
- ▶ mountain

Other ideas

- ▶ Put some blue or green food colouring in the water.
- ▶ Drop food colouring into the ice cube trays before freezing and watch what happens.
- ▶ Load the icebergs and try to sink them.

Songs and stories

- ▶ Pingu
- ▶ Tacky the Penguin
- ▶ Row, Row, Row your Boat
- ▶ Ebb and Flo
- ▶ Penguins in the Fridge
- ▶ We're going on a Bear Hunt (you could make up your own polar bear version!)
- ▶ Non-fiction books about cold countries

See it grow

Many things will grow in water alone. Try some hydroponics with the children (growing plants without soil) and watch as your seedlings develop!

Contribution to Early Learning Goals

PRIME

Communication and language
① Listening and attention
② Understanding
③ Speaking

Physical development
① Moving and handling

Personal, social and emotional development
① Self-confidence and self-awareness
② Managing feelings and behaviour
③ Making relationships

SPECIFIC

Mathematics
② Shape, space and measures

Understanding of the world
① People and communities
② The world

What you need:

- ▶ clear plastic bottles
- ▶ seeds, pips, beans
- ▶ cotton wool, wadding or old socks
- ▶ labels and pens
- ▶ magnifying glasses
- ▶ perlite, peat moss or gravel

Rinse each plastic bottle, draw a line with a marker pen around the middle and cut the bottle in two. Cut a section of wadding, cotton wool or from an old sock, and use this material to fully block the neck of the bottle. Fill the bottom half of the bottle with water, and rest the top half upside down so that the wadding in the bottleneck is sitting in the water. Fill the top with your medium (perlite, peat moss or gravel) and plant the seeds. Label each bottle if using different types of seed. Moisten the seeds in the medium with a cup of water. Watch your plants grow!

Vocabulary

- ▶ grow
- ▶ soil
- ▶ gravel
- ▶ water
- ▶ rain
- ▶ sun
- ▶ damp
- ▶ cold

- ▶ warm
- ▶ magnifying glass
- ▶ dig
- ▶ pour
- ▶ label
- ▶ watch
- ▶ plant
- ▶ time

- ▶ how long
- ▶ how many
- ▶ measure
- ▶ bulbs
- ▶ seeds
- ▶ sprout

Other ideas

- ▶ Grow beans or peas in jars lined with blotting paper.
- ▶ Grow cress hair in egg shells stuffed with wet cotton wool and decorated with crayon faces.
- ▶ Fill your water tray or a bowl with water, sand and pond plants.

Songs and stories

- ▶ The Seed
- ▶ Titch
- ▶ Mary, Mary, Quite Contrary
- ▶ Jack and the Beanstalk

Moving waters

There are many ways of making water move. You can use mechanical methods or child power! Some of these ways to make water move are better done outside!

Contribution to Early Learning Goals

PRIME

Communication and language
1. Listening and attention
2. Understanding
3. Speaking

Physical development
1. Moving and handling

Personal, social and emotional development
1. Self-confidence and self-awareness
2. Managing feelings and behaviour

SPECIFIC

Mathematics
2. Shape, space and measures

Understanding of the world
1. People and communities
2. The world

Expressive arts and design
1. Exploring and using media and materials

What you need:

- tubes of all sorts
- guttering and drainpipes
- water wheels
- siphons
- pumps
- Aqualab or other water construction sets
- hoses of different lengths

- funnels
- scoops
- plastic bottles
- washing-up liquid
- bubbles
- ping pong balls
- little boats
- bricks for propping

I will need

Vocabulary

- pump
- pour
- trickle
- down/up
- fill
- funnel
- flow
- bubble

- lift
- turn
- through
- move
- spray
- full/empty
- high/low
- in/out

- fast/slow
- lock
- gate
- block
- suck/blow
- push/pull
- float/sink

Other ideas

- Try some garden sprays, with or without paint in the water.
- Experiment with locks and canals in plastic guttering.
- Look at pet drinking bottles.
- Use straws or fans to race boats or ping pong balls.

Songs and stories

- Rosie and Jim
- The Cow Who Fell in the Canal
- Waterfalls and Canal Boats
- The Pig in the Pond

- Master Plug the Plumber
- Fact books about water, water wheels and plumbing

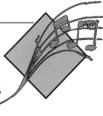

Float or sink?

Experiments with floating and sinking are part of scientific learning. Use your water tray to find out about and observe how materials behave in water. Sort, predict, explore and discuss.

Contribution to Early Learning Goals

PRIME

Communication and language
(1) Listening and attention
(2) Understanding
(3) Speaking

Physical development
(1) Moving and handling

Personal, social and emotional development
(1) Self-confidence and self-awareness
(2) Managing feelings and behaviour
(3) Making relationships

SPECIFIC

Mathematics
(2) Shape, space and measures

Understanding of the world
(1) People and communities
(2) The world

Expressive arts and design
(1) Exploring and using media and materials
(2) Being imaginative

What you need:

- a plank or shelf to put across the tray (to use for resting things on)
- containers of water, preferably transparent (deep enough to see if things are really sinking or just floating beneath the surface)
- objects made from wood, plastic, metal, sponge etc.

- stones, shells, seeds
- fruit and vegetables
- fabric, plastic and paper
- feathers, leaves and flowers
- plastic and foil dishes
- boats and other floating containers
- whiteboards

Vocabulary

float	heavy	predict
sink	absorb	guess
under	dissolve	right
bottom	above	wrong
soaking	below	why?
surface	full	decide
different	empty	watch
light	think	collect

Other ideas

- Offer some waterproof recording sheets or picture labels so the children can record their findings.
- Make boats and load them to see how they work.
- Go to the park and play Pooh Sticks.

Songs and stories

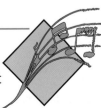

- The Little Boat
- You Can Swim, Jim
- Noah's Ark
- The Big Ship Sails

- Mr Gumpy's Outing
- Non-fiction books about boats

Washing day

Set up your own laundry day or car wash and recreate familiar water-based experiences.

Contribution to Early Learning Goals
PRIME
Communication and language
- (1) Listening and attention
- (2) Understanding
- (3) Speaking

Physical development
- (1) Moving and handling
- (2) Health and self-care

Personal, social and emotional development
- (1) Self-confidence and self-awareness
- (2) Managing feelings and behaviour
- (3) Making relationships

SPECIFIC
Understanding of the world
- (1) People and communities

What you need:

For a laundry day:

▶ washing-up bowls

▶ a clothes line and pegs

▶ warm water and soap (check for allergies, and avoid harsh detergents)

▶ waterproof table cover

▶ plastic crockery, dolls clothes and dolls

For a car wash:

▶ wheeled toys

▶ buckets and sponges

▶ clipboards

▶ plastic or real money

▶ tickets or tokens

▶ wellington boots

▶ rubber gloves

▶ playground chalk

Vocabulary

▶ wash	▶ bubbles	▶ number
▶ clean	▶ hang	▶ ticket/token
▶ dirty	▶ iron	▶ foam
▶ bath	▶ squeeze	▶ next
▶ peg	▶ pay	▶ turn
▶ wet	▶ wait	▶ finished
▶ dry	▶ line	▶ ready
▶ dripping	▶ money	▶ polish

Other ideas:

▶ Spring clean your setting and wash all the washable apparatus.

▶ Set up a window cleaning service or decorator.

▶ Make an underwater grotto with fish and mermaids.

▶ Have a swimming pool or beach with a café.

Songs and stories

▶ A Sailor went to Sea, Sea, Sea

▶ The Big Ship Sails

▶ Row, Row, Row your Boat

▶ The Lighthouse Keeper's Lunch

▶ The Little Boat

▶ Master Salt the Sailor

▶ Sailor Bear

Water in the kitchen

Involve the children in exploring the uses of water in cooking, mixing, diluting and boiling, from diluting squash or making a cup of tea to jellies, lollies and ice cubes.

Contribution to Early Learning Goals

PRIME

Communication and language
1. Listening and attention
2. Understanding
3. Speaking

Physical development
1. Moving and handling

Personal, social and emotional development
1. Self-confidence and self-awareness
2. Managing feelings and behaviour
3. Making relationships

SPECIFIC

Mathematics
1. Numbers
2. Shape, space and measures

Understanding of the world
2. The world

What you need:

For ice lollies:

▶ moulds

▶ sticks

▶ fruit juices diluted with water

For fruit cubes:

▶ ice cube trays

▶ small fruit (e.g. blueberries, raspberries, tangerine slices)

For jelly:

▶ packet jelly

▶ mixing jug

▶ hot water (adult only)

▶ moulds (e.g. cups, yogurt pots, muffin moulds, polystyrene cups and shape moulds)

Vocabulary

▶ mix	▶ change	▶ wait
▶ stir	▶ powder	▶ thick
▶ pour	▶ liquid	▶ soft
▶ dissolve	▶ solid	▶ touch
▶ hot	▶ yolk	▶ taste
▶ cold	▶ white	▶ smooth
▶ freeze	▶ boil	▶ lumpy
▶ set	▶ count	▶ different

Other ideas

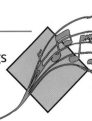

▶ Boil or poach some eggs. (Add a teaspoon of vinegar to the poaching water to help the eggs stay together.)

▶ Scrub and peel vegetables, then boil (adult-only step) and mash them.

▶ Make jelly in a flat baking tray and cut out shapes with cutters.

Songs and stories

▶ Jelly on the Plate

▶ Someone's in the Kitchen

▶ Chick, Chick Chicken

▶ Oliver's Vegetables

▶ Variations on other songs (e.g. Ten red ice cubes sitting in the fridge)

It's raining

Don't let the rain stop you having fun outside. Cover up or get an umbrella and find out about the rain. Even if you can't all go out at once, small groups can explore outside.

Contribution to Early Learning Goals
PRIME
Communication and language
1. Listening and attention
2. Understanding
3. Speaking

Physical development
1. Moving and handling
2. Health and self-care

Personal, social and emotional development
1. Self-confidence and self-awareness
2. Managing feelings and behaviour
3. Making relationships

SPECIFIC
Understanding of the world
2. The world

What you need:

- umbrellas (different sizes, colours and types)
- wellington boots
- raincoats
- pop-up tents and tunnels
- plastic bottles and funnels for rain gauges
- sieves, colanders and nets
- clear plastic sheeting to make shelters

- mirrors
- whiteboards or clipboards with waterproof pens
- magnifying glasses
- scoops and sticks to explore puddles
- playground chalk

Vocabulary

- rain
- shower
- raindrop
- drizzle
- pouring
- cloud
- soaking
- drenched

- shelter
- wet/dry
- listen
- splash
- puddle
- thunder
- collect
- watch

- evaporate
- floating
- trickle
- drip
- forecast
- sky
- blowing
- falling

Other ideas

- Explore puddles by puddle jumping, splashing, poking with sticks and dipping.
- Make weather charts.
- Use droppers or straws with water, paint or food colouring on wet paper.
- Put a pop-up tent just outside the door, in the rain.

Songs and stories

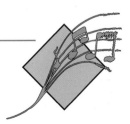

- It's Raining, It's Pouring
- Rain, Rain, Go Away

- I Hear Thunder
- Noah's Ark

Add something

Adding anything to water is a great experiment. Investigate with adding colour, other liquids, powders, soil, sand, and bubbles. Be adventurous and explore what happens. Encourage the children to predict what they think will happen.

Contribution to Early Learning Goals

PRIME

Communication and language
(1) Listening and attention
(2) Understanding
(3) Speaking

Physical development
(1) Moving and handling

Personal, social and emotional development
(1) Self-confidence and self-awareness
(2) Managing feelings and behaviour

SPECIFIC

Understanding of the world
(2) The world

Expressive arts and design
(1) Exploring and using media and materials

What you need:

- water and containers
- spoons
- droppers
- whisks
- straws
- bubble blowers
- food colouring
- sugar
- cellulose paste

- salt
- mud
- flour
- glue
- jelly crystals
- soap
- sand
- clay
- dry pasta or rice

Vocabulary

- think
- right
- happen
- pour
- tip
- mix
- stir
- whisk

- sink
- dissolve
- disappear
- clear
- cloudy
- pale
- thick
- wait

- separate
- layers
- top/bottom
- surface
- soft
- bubbles
- burst
- colours

Other ideas

- Print with tissue or crêpe paper dipped in water.
- Mix salt or sugar in paint to make sparkly pictures.
- Make papier-mâché.
- Add water to clay and use for painting on the ground outside (the rain will wash it away!).

Songs and stories

- Simple science books

31

Full and empty

Begin these science-based activities with plenty of free play before intervening and influencing the activities. Make sure you have plenty of different sized and shaped containers, scoops and spoons.

Contribution to Early Learning Goals

PRIME

Communication and language
① Listening and attention
② Understanding
③ Speaking

Physical development
① Moving and handling

Personal, social and emotional development
① Self-confidence and self-awareness
② Managing feelings and behaviour

SPECIFIC

Mathematics
① Numbers
② Shape, space and measures

Understanding of the world
② The world

Expressive arts and design
① Exploring and using media and materials

What you need:

- a water tray, bath or other receptacle
- a board or bath rack at one end will make a shelf to put things on
- whiteboards and clipboards and pens
- spoons
- scoops
- jugs
- cups and mugs
- plastic bottles in various sizes (try to get some very small ones as well as big ones)
- funnels
- beads or marbles for tallying and counting

Vocabulary

- count
- how many
- empty
- half full
- full
- pour
- big
- small
- top
- bottom
- more
- less
- bigger
- smaller
- size
- shape
- inside
- spill
- overflow
- record
- write
- number
- board

Other ideas

- Visit a supermarket and look at measures on labels.
- Collect some containers and use waterproof markers to record changing water levels.
- Fill bottles with varying volumes of water, and blow across the tops to create your own harmonica.
- Collect some glass bottles, all the same size. Fill them with coloured water to different levels. Hang them up or stand them on a board. Tap the bottles gently with a stick or beater to make a tune.

Songs and stories

- Ten Green Bottles
- Simple science books

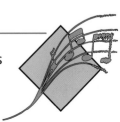

Water in the garden

The garden is an ideal place to have fun with water. Be creative and use it in tubes, guttering, ponds and pools. Try a making a bird bath, waterfall or a fountain. Paint with water, throw it, spray it, splash in it and paddle in it!

Contribution to Early Learning Goals

PRIME

Communication and language
1. Listening and attention
2. Understanding
3. Speaking

Physical development
1. Moving and handling

Personal, social and emotional development
1. Self-confidence and self-awareness
2. Managing feelings and behaviour
3. Making relationships

SPECIFIC

Understanding of the world
2. The world

What you need:

- plastic sheeting or pond liner
- stones and rocks
- guttering, tubes and pipes
- hose
- buckets
- tubs and containers for ponds
- pond plants and fish
- watering can

For fun in the garden:

- water bombs
- paddling pools
- sponge balls
- water pistols
- bubbles and blowers
- plastic fish, frogs and ducks
- old towels

I will need

Vocabulary

- fill
- watering can
- carry
- heavy
- stones
- leak
- overflow
- deep
- shallow

- fun
- throw
- splash
- splat
- spray
- squish
- pour
- game
- soak

- laugh
- surprise
- paddle
- feet/toes
- trick
- dry
- towel

Other ideas

- Make a little pond or a bird bath in an upturned dustbin lid propped up with stones or bricks.
- Make a rill (small stream) using plastic guttering all the way round the garden. Float boats in it.
- Make a bubble fountain using stones and a hose.

Safety hints

Remember that ponds and pools are dangerous places for small children – they should be carefully supervised and made as safe as possible.

Edges of raised pools should be above children's waist level. Bigger ponds should be covered with secure netting or grills (under the surface looks better!).

At the beach

Traditional sand tray activities give children plenty of enjoyable practice of filling, emptying, building and exploring this medium. Children need plenty of free experience of this sort before and between more directed sand activities.

Contribution to Early Learning Goals

PRIME

Communication and language
1. Listening and attention
2. Understanding
3. Speaking

Physical development
1. Moving and handling

Personal, social and emotional development
1. Self-confidence and self-awareness
2. Managing feelings and behaviour
3. Making relationships

SPECIFIC

Understanding of the world
1. People and communities
2. The world

Expressive arts and design
1. Exploring and using media and materials
2. Being imaginative

What you need:

- sand tray with dry or damp sand
- buckets
- spades
- sand moulds
- plastic cups, trays
- plastic bottles
- scoops
- sand rakes
- spoons
- shells
- pebbles
- plastic sea creatures

Vocabulary

- sand
- bury
- pat
- heavy
- upside down
- collapse
- slide
- fill
- tip
- dig
- build
- castle
- moat
- turret
- tower
- bridge
- tunnel
- gate
- pool
- beach
- rock pool
- seaside
- salty
- tide

Other ideas

- Offer some paper and small sticks to make flags.
- Collect seaside pictures.
- Make sand pictures (colour sand by putting it in zip lock bags and adding paint or food colouring).
- Turn your role play area into an ice cream parlour.

Songs and stories

- Sally and the Limpet
- Ebb and Flo
- The Lighthouse Keeper's Lunch
- The Little Boat
- I Went to Visit the Beach One Day
- Daddy's Taking Us to the Beach Tomorrow (Daddy's Taking Us to the Zoo Tomorrow)

Hot, hot, hot!

Create a desert in your sand tray or in any shallow container. Make an oasis with trees, animals and people. Make sand dunes, add a river or some houses and tents. Concentrate on animals that like hot places – snakes, lizards, spiders etc.

Contribution to Early Learning Goals

PRIME

Communication and language
1. Listening and attention
2. Understanding
3. Speaking

Physical development
1. Moving and handling

Personal, social and emotional development
1. Self-confidence and self-awareness
2. Managing feelings and behaviour
3. Making relationships

SPECIFIC

Understanding of the world
1. People and communities
2. The world

Expressive arts and design
1. Exploring and using media and materials
2. Being imaginative

What you need:

- a sand tray or shallow container
- dry or damp sand
- toy camels, donkeys etc.
- small world people
- trucks and other vehicles
- palm trees
- foil, tin lids or plastic mirrors for water or rivers

For animal habitats:
- toy snakes
- toy lizards
- toy spiders
- toy centipedes
- toy scorpions
- toy ants

I will need

Vocabulary

- boiling
- hat
- shorts
- sunshade
- glasses
- shelter
- dry
- water

- sand dune
- adventure
- thirsty
- driver
- stuck
- night
- rescue
- oasis

- camp
- tent
- sandstorm
- camel
- ride
- expedition

Other ideas:

- Make a role-play backpack for explorers in the desert.
- Look at atlases and globes to find hot places.
- Hang a thermometer outside and check temperatures.
- Make desert pictures.

Songs and stories

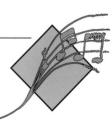

- Books about deserts and living in hot countries.
- Animal and reptile books.
- Change the words to the song 'Over in the Meadow': 'Over in the desert, in the sand, in the sun, lived an old mother lizard and her little baby one...'

Digger

Most children love watching and playing with diggers, dumper trucks and tipper lorries. Use these in sand trays or shallow containers of sand or gravel. This activity can be linked to a topic on construction or vehicles.

Contribution to Early Learning Goals

PRIME

Communication and language
1. Listening and attention
2. Understanding
3. Speaking

Physical development
1. Moving and handling

Personal, social and emotional development
1. Self-confidence and self-awareness
2. Managing feelings and behaviour
3. Making relationships

SPECIFIC

Understanding of the world
1. People and communities
2. The world

Expressive arts and design
1. Exploring and using media and materials
2. Being imaginative

What you need:

- a sand tray or shallow container
- diggers
- dumper trucks
- tipper trucks
- cranes
- lorries
- small bags or sacks
- small world people

- chalk
- clipboards and pens
- paper, card, sticks for labels and signs
- sand
- gravel
- pebbles
- sieves (to sieve the stones out of the sand)

Vocabulary

- dig
- tip
- pour
- fill
- drive/driver
- deliver
- order
- building

- making
- driving
- reversing
- signal
- careful
- shovel
- gravel
- cement

- construction
- hard hat
- tea break
- sandwiches
- instructions
- boss
- builder
- flashing

Other ideas

- Make a building site outside with hard hats, wheeled toys etc.
- Put some big stones and wheelbarrows in the garden. Let the children shift them and pile them up.
- Visit a local building site or builders merchant.

Songs and stories

- Bob the Builder DVDs
- The Building Site
- Miss Brick the Builder
- Peter Hammers

- Non-fiction books about lorries, cranes and diggers
- Sing 'The Wheels on the Truck go Round and Round'

Dinosaur land

Transform your sand tray into a prehistoric land, or prepare to be archaeologists by excavating buried 'bones' or 'fossils'!

Contribution to Early Learning Goals

PRIME

Communication and language
1. Listening and attention
2. Understanding
3. Speaking

Physical development
1. Moving and handling

Personal, social and emotional development
1. Self-confidence and self-awareness
2. Managing feelings and behaviour
3. Making relationships

SPECIFIC

Understanding of the world
1. People and communities
2. The world

Expressive arts and design
2. Being imaginative

What you need:

- plastic dinosaurs
- sand
- stones
- gravel
- a shallow container of water for a lake
- trees
- card, stiff plastic etc. to support caves
- 'bones' made from plastic, polystyrene or baked dough
- 'fossils' made by pressing objects into plasticine/clay
- brushes, trowels, sieves spades and magnifying glasses
- notebooks and pens
- cameras (real or pretend)

Vocabulary

- dinosaur
- fossil
- ancient
- long ago
- prehistoric
- fierce
- meat eaters
- plant eaters
- extinct
- scientist
- museum
- excavate
- film/video
- television
- bones
- hammer
- rocks
- stegosaurus
- tyrannosaurus
- diplodocus
- triceratops
- pterodactyl
- iguanodon
- brontosaurus

Other ideas:

- Make dinosaur 'footprints' in modelling clay.
- Look for prints of birds and animals in the garden.
- Make up a dance and move like dinosaurs.
- Use chalk or paint to draw dinosaurs on big paper or on the ground outside.

Songs and stories

- Listen to the Chorus
- Dinosaur Roar
- Harry and the Bucket of Dinosaurs
- Dinosaur Dinners
- Long Neck and Thunder Foot
- Dinosaur Encyclopedia
- Prehistoric World

Animals everywhere

Farm and zoo animals are always favourites in the sand tray. Sort the animals so the different types are kept separate. Include fences, gates and cages to make farms and zoos.

Contribution to Early Learning Goals

PRIME

Communication and language
1. Listening and attention
2. Understanding
3. Speaking

Physical development
1. Moving and handling

Personal, social and emotional development
1. Self-confidence and self-awareness
2. Managing feelings and behaviour
3. Making relationships

SPECIFIC

Mathematics
1. Numbers
2. Shape, space and measures

Understanding of the world
1. People and communities
2. The world

Expressive arts and design
1. Exploring and using media and materials
2. Being imaginative

What you need:

- farm animals
- zoo animals
- fences
- gates
- gravel for paths
- mirrors or silver foil for ponds, streams and rivers
- tractors and other farm vehicles
- miniature trees
- signs and labels
- small world people

Vocabulary

- animal
- zoo
- farm
- farmer
- feed
- collect
- babies
- live

- water
- land
- drink
- nest
- carry
- plant
- harvest
- zoo keeper

- country
- jungle
- river
- pond
- field
- forest
- visitors
- market

Other ideas

- Make animals from recycled materials.
- Use chalk to make a big farm or zoo layout on the path, playground or a huge sheet of paper.

Songs and stories

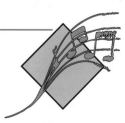

- I Went to Visit a Farm/Zoo One Day
- Old McDonald had a Farm/Zoo
- I Went to the Animal Fair
- Dear Zoo
- Elmer the Patchwork Elephant
- Fact books, encyclopedias, DVDs

Sieve, funnel and tube

Collect all the equipment you have for pouring, tipping, sieving and shifting sand. Put a board across the sand tray to create more room to work. You could mark the board with 'shadows' of the equipment to make clearing up easier!

Contribution to Early Learning Goals

PRIME

Communication and language
① Listening and attention
② Understanding
③ Speaking

Physical development
① Moving and handling

Personal, social and emotional development
① Self-confidence and self-awareness
② Managing feelings and behaviour
③ Making relationships

SPECIFIC

Mathematics
② Shape, space and measures

Understanding of the world
② The world

What you need:

- dry sand
- funnels
- scoops and spoons
- plastic tubing
- plastic bottles
- jugs
- sieves and strainers
- drainpipes
- guttering

- sand wheels
- pulleys
- cranes
- gravel
- small stones and pebbles
- string
- small containers
- lorries and tippers
- small sacks and bags

I will need

Vocabulary

- pour
- tip
- roll
- fill
- empty
- lift
- scoop

- lever
- tubes
- fall
- through
- funnel
- bottle
- carry

- mix
- deliver
- turn
- steady
- help
- together

Other ideas

- Take the sand outside and make giant constructions for moving sand through tubes and funnels. Make it go right across the garden, down from the climbing frame, or from a wall or fence. Plastic guttering is good for this activity.

Songs and stories

- The Building Site

Make your own versions of songs, e.g.

- Lift, lift, lift the sand,
  Lift it with the crane,
  Lifting it, lifting it,
  Lifting it, lifting it,
  Lifting with the crane.

(To 'Row, Row, Row your Boat')

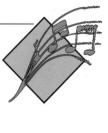

- The sand in the wheel goes round and round round and round round and round. The sand in the wheel goes round and round All day long.

(To `The Wheels on the Bus').

47

Mould and shape

Damp sand behaves in a very different way from dry sand. Provide a collection of implements and moulds, and let children explore the patterns and shapes they can make with damp sand.

Contribution to Early Learning Goals

PRIME

Communication and language
1. Listening and attention
2. Understanding
3. Speaking

Physical development
1. Moving and handling

Personal, social and emotional development
1. Self-confidence and self-awareness
2. Managing feelings and behaviour
3. Making relationships

SPECIFIC

Mathematics
2. Shape, space and measures

Understanding of the world
2. The world

Expressive arts and design
1. Exploring and using media and materials
2. Being imaginative

What you need:

- buckets of different shapes and sizes
- bun and muffin trays
- sand moulds
- spades, spoons and scoops
- rakes and forks
- cups and mugs

- shape cutters
- objects to press into the sand and use for decoration – shells, plastic toys, nuts and seeds, dry pasta, flowers, leaves and sticks
- materials to make flags

I will need

Vocabulary

press	stand	track
pat	crumble	count
hard	fall	flag
mould	decorate	door
castle	tower	cakes
marks	turret	party
empty	print	enough
stick	mark	choose

Other ideas

- Colour some of the sand by putting it in a zip-lock bag with food colouring or paint and shaking or squeezing it.
- Make a huge castle outside on the ground or in a cement mixing tray.

Add it!

Add things to dry sand and have fun finding them and getting them out again. The youngest children will need supervision with small objects for health and safety reasons.

Contribution to Early Learning Goals

PRIME

Communication and language
1. Listening and attention
2. Understanding
3. Speaking

Physical development
1. Moving and handling

Personal, social and emotional development
1. Self-confidence and self-awareness
2. Managing feelings and behaviour
3. Making relationships

SPECIFIC

Understanding of the world
2. The world

Expressive arts and design
1. Exploring and using media and materials

What you need:

▶ dry sand

Things to add:

▶ different sized beads

▶ dry pasta, rice and beans

▶ sequins or glitter

▶ screws, nuts and bolts

▶ shavings

▶ very small toys, animals etc.

▶ stones and pebbles

Things to get them out with:

▶ sieves, colanders and netting

▶ small fishing nets

▶ tea strainers or slotted spoons

▶ tweezers

▶ plastic/metal tongs

▶ magnets

Vocabulary

▶ surface
▶ buried
▶ mixed
▶ disappear
▶ small
▶ sieve
▶ shake
▶ separate

▶ find
▶ discover
▶ sort
▶ challenge
▶ fingers
▶ tweezers
▶ tongs
▶ squeeze

▶ careful
▶ lift
▶ fall
▶ holes
▶ help
▶ together
▶ hold
▶ problem

Other ideas

▶ Mix several objects into the sand (e.g. screws, sequins and beads) and set a challenge of getting each type of object out using a different tool.

▶ Using individual sand trays and tweezers or tongs helps develop fine motor skills.

Songs and stories

▶ Fact books about magnets

You could sing different words for:

▶ Pop Goes the Weasel

▶ Mix a Pancake

▶ Roll the Bobbin

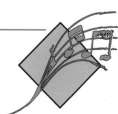

Sand art

Sand is a very good medium for art work of all sorts. You can add things to it, sculpt it, drizzle it and stick it onto things. You can make coloured sand for pictures and structures, you can sprinkle it, spread it, and explore it with your hands!

Contribution to Early Learning Goals

PRIME

Communication and language
1. Listening and attention
2. Understanding
3. Speaking

Physical development
1. Moving and handling

Personal, social and emotional development
1. Self-confidence and self-awareness
2. Managing feelings and behaviour
3. Making relationships

SPECIFIC

Literacy
1. Writing

Understanding of the world
2. The world

Expressive arts and design
1. Exploring and using media and materials
2. Being imaginative

What you need:

- fine dry silver sand
- spoons
- scoops
- plastic or butter knives
- brushes
- plastic gloves

Additional materials:

- perfumed oils
- paint: powder, liquid and finger
- white glue (makes sand shiny and dries hard for sculptures)
- food colouring
- glitter or salt (makes sand sparkly)

- sawdust (makes sand grainy)
- small plastic bags
- paper and card
- table covering

Vocabulary

mix	hard	sticky
drizzle	soft	sparkly
drip	model	shiny
pour	sculpture	gritty
paint	colour	stiff
smooth	smell	decorate
rough	perfume	keep
lumpy	liquid	drying

Other ideas

- Mix sand, soil and glue to make real mud pies.
- Put dry sand in a plastic bag or a glove, make a little hole and use to make trail pictures (indoors or out).
- Paint with glue and sprinkle with sand. Shake off excess sand.

Make it permanent

Mix sand with cement to make permanent features for your garden or playground. It is important for children to wear goggles when mixing cement, and gloves when handling wet cement.

Contribution to Early Learning Goals

PRIME

Communication and language
1. Listening and attention
2. Understanding
3. Speaking

Physical development
1. Moving and handling

Personal, social and emotional development
1. Self-confidence and self-awareness
2. Managing feelings and behaviour
3. Making relationships

SPECIFIC

Understanding of the world
2. The world

Expressive arts and design
1. Exploring and using media and materials
2. Being imaginative

What you need:

This activity is best done outside, and with a hose for cleaning up!

- builder's sand
- cement
- cement mixing tray
- small spades or shovels
- buckets
- goggles, coveralls and gloves

- moulds such as large lids from paint cans, flat boxes, old trays etc.
- shells, stones, flowers seeds etc. to press into cement
- rakes, forks, toy cars, buttons etc. to make textures and patterns
- sticks, old pencils etc.

I will need

Vocabulary

- mix
- pour
- builder
- spade
- add
- measure
- sand
- cement

- hard
- mould
- shape
- stay
- decorate
- choose
- permanent
- outside

- feel
- touch
- stand
- walk
- hop
- jump
- fix
- forever

Other ideas

Using sand and cement

- Using cement is a great idea. It creates something permanent for your setting and can be personalised by children, using sticks to write their names and pressing hands and feet into the wet cement.

- The cement can be made into paving stones, or stepping stones. It can also be used to make plaques and tiles for walls and seating areas.

- You can use sand mixed with peat and treated cement to make rocks for pools or gardens, and even decorative troughs and planters. NB. Untreated cement is toxic to fish.

Sand dough

Sand is such a versatile medium, and here are even more ideas for using it! Try making sand dough. It will harden over a few days, but would be quicker in a very low oven (not a microwave!).

Contribution to Early Learning Goals

PRIME

Communication and language
(1) Listening and attention
(2) Understanding
(3) Speaking

Physical development
(1) Moving and handling

Personal, social and emotional development
(1) Self-confidence and self-awareness
(2) Managing feelings and behaviour
(3) Making relationships

SPECIFIC

Understanding of the world
(2) The world

Expressive arts and design
(1) Exploring and using media and materials
(2) Being imaginative

What you need:

This makes a large amount – halve the quantities if you like.

- 4.5kg (10lb) of flour
- 2.5L (10 cups) of water
- 1.25L (5 cups) of sand
- about 1 cup of white glue
- one big sheet or several small sheets of hardboard or plywood
- paint and brushes
- a big plastic bowl or bucket
- plastic bags
- plastic sheet
- sticks, blunt knives etc. for moulding

Keep spare dough sealed in a plastic bag to keep it soft.

Vocabulary

mix	sand	fingers
pour	stir	feel
build	dry	touch
spoon	shape	dough
add	cover	paint
measure	decorate	colour
weigh	help	together
flour	hands	group

What you do:

1. Put the flour and sand in the bowl and mix thoroughly.

2. Add the water until you have made a stiff dough. Children will enjoy this, but may need some help with stirring.

3. Roll up your sleeves and knead the dough with your hands until all lumps have gone.

4. Take a lump of dough each and shape a figure, animal or other shape.

5. Leave to dry, paint, then varnish with diluted white glue.

You could make a group sculpture!

Sock of sand

This activity is great fun and will encourage hand-eye co-ordination. It is messy though – so be warned and cover up! It is best undertaken outside.

Contribution to Early Learning Goals

PRIME

Communication and language
1. Listening and attention
2. Understanding
3. Speaking

Physical development
1. Moving and handling

Personal, social and emotional development
1. Self-confidence and self-awareness
2. Managing feelings and behaviour
3. Making relationships

SPECIFIC

Understanding of the world
2. The world

Expressive arts and design
1. Exploring and using media and materials
2. Being imaginative

What you need:

- old tights (adult-size if possible)
- dry sand
- funnel
- small spades or shovels
- paint and paint pots or trays, at least 3cm deep

- several colours of fairly thick paint
- aprons
- table covers
- large sheets of paper on a table or the floor

Vocabulary

sock	careful	spread
paint	enough	colour
fill	dip	pattern
tie	slap	careful
knot	drop	enjoy
drizzle	drip	high
sand	splash	

What you do:

1. Cut the legs off the tights (leaving a long length to tie).

2. Help the children to fill the tight socks until the sand is about the size of their fist.

3. Tie a knot in the sock or tight as close to the sand as possible (leaving some of the sock to hold on to).

4. Put some paint in shallow pans and fix some paper to a table or the floor.

5. Dip the sand socks into the paint and slap or drop them on the paper. Use a different sock for each colour.

Skittles

Use sand to make your own game of skittles. This activity gives children a good opportunity to use counting in a practical situation. Offer them a small white board or clipboard for scoring – or playground chalk to write on the wall or ground.

Contribution to Early Learning Goals

PRIME

Communication and language
① Listening and attention
② Understanding
③ Speaking

Physical development
① Moving and handling

Personal, social and emotional development
① Self-confidence and self-awareness
② Managing feelings and behaviour
③ Making relationships

SPECIFIC

Mathematics
① Numbers

What you need:

- sand
- plastic bottles from water or other drinks 6 for a set
- funnel
- newspaper
- PVA glue
- paints
- wool for hair
- paint brushes
- soft balls
- clip boards or whiteboards
- playground chalk

Vocabulary

- funnel
- pour
- bottle
- careful
- scrunch
- stick
- dry
- paint
- tear
- colours
- pattern
- face
- hair
- play
- turns
- outside
- throw
- fall
- score
- stand

What you do:

1. Help the children to fill each bottle about one third full with sand.

2. Scrunch a piece of paper into a ball, and wrap the ball in two sheets of paper, leaving some loose to push into the bottle as a neck.

3. Stick the neck into the bottle and secure with pasted strips of newspaper over the join and down the bottle.

4. Cover the whole bottle with paper strips and PVA glue, and leave to dry.

5. Paint the bottle with patterns, or paint on clothes, make a face and add some wool hair. For older children, paint a score on each bottle.

6. Stand the skittles up and roll a soft ball to play. Score if you want.

Coloured sand jars

Alum Bay in the Isle of Wight was the original holiday resort for these souvenirs, which are filled with layers of different coloured sand. The children can make their own with a bit of help from you.

Contribution to Early Learning Goals

PRIME

Communication and language
(1) Listening and attention
(2) Understanding
(3) Speaking

Physical development
(1) Moving and handling

Personal, social and emotional development
(1) Self-confidence and self-awareness
(2) Managing feelings and behaviour
(3) Making relationships

SPECIFIC

Understanding of the world
(2) The world

Expressive arts and design
(1) Exploring and using media and materials
(2) Being imaginative

What you need:

- dry sand
- funnels
- powder or tempera paint
- small zip-lock plastic bags
- shallow baking tins
- small spoons
- small plastic or glass jars with lids (baby food jars are good)

- tape or a glue gun to seal jars (adult use only!)
- paint with white glue added (to decorate the lids)
- small brushes or cotton buds

Vocabulary

- pour
- mix
- colour
- stir
- bake
- dry

- hot
- choose
- layers
- different
- steady
- careful

- stick
- paint
- present
- undo

What you do:

1. Help them to pour some sand into several different plastic bags.

2. Add several teaspoons of paint to each bag, seal and squeeze until the paint is well mixed with the sand.

3. Tip the coloured sand onto the baking trays and leave to dry in a warm place or a low oven (not a microwave!).

4. Using small spoons, help the children to layer the coloured sands into the jars, until the jar is completely full (don't leave any space or the colours will mix up if the jar is tipped).

5. Screw the top on and seal with tape or a glue gun (adult only).

6. Decorate the lid with paint and white glue.

The Little Books Club

There is always something in Little Books to help and inspire you. Packed full of lovely ideas, Little Books meet the need for exciting and practical activities that are fun to do, address the Early Learning Goals and can be followed in most settings. Everyone is a winner!

We publish 5 new Little Books a year. Little Books Club members receive each of these 5 books as soon as they are published for a reduced price. The subscription cost is £29.99 – a one off payment that buys the 5 new books for £4.99 instead of £8.99 each.

In addition to this, Little Books Club Members receive:
- Free postage and packing on anything ordered from the Featherstone catalogue
- A 15% discount voucher upon joining which can be used to buy any number of books from the Featherstone catalogue
- Members price of £4.99 on any additional Little Book purchased
- A regular, free newsletter dealing with club news, special offers and aspects of Early Years curriculum and practice
- All new Little Books on approval - return in good condition within 30 days and we'll refund the cost to your club account

Call 020 7758 0200 or email: littlebooks@bloomsbury.com for an enrolment pack. Or download an application form from our website:

www.bloomsbury.com